Interrupted Verse:
Collected Poetry 2016-2019

Interrupted Verse:
Collected Poetry 2016-2019

Derek Des Anges

House of D Publications
2020

First Printing: 2020

ISBN: 978-0-244-24293-0

House of D Publications, London

Dedication

For Kasper, and everyone else we lost; for Emma, and everyone else who lost someone.

Contents

Introduction 1

Poems 3
   do nothing..3
   last quarter before the equinox 4
   bath salts 5
   urban planning & the enclosure act
....7
   Fresh stigmata 9
   What we leave behind 12
   it was summer..................................14
   two languages 15
   safe house 19
   the last runner 21
   old world genealogy........................24
   only you can prevent 25
   woodsman 26
   tourist tout 28
   the penitent wife 32
   appetites 33
   Baphomet 35
   The Map-Maker's Lament on Losing
His Daughter 36
   Migrate or Die 38
   Hard Bastard 39
   forgotten feelings............................40

that martha stewart feeling...........41
identity cards and the body politic
....43
can you feel me dancing 46
memory is rewritten, not recalled
....48
cypress path.......................................50
give up your love poems.................51
too realistic for poetry 53
more life...55
hillier's remnants 56
What goes around...............................59
There's no escaping the maze
without a lamp 60
recruitment drive 62
far from damascus (attempt 1) 63
unWanton...64
Like Father, Not Sun.........................65
silhouettes in an east london flat 67
temporal lobe seizure 69
greenery from blackening 72
valley of long-forgotten kings.......74
credon't...75
message from the gods.....................76
i have no time for romance............77
global 78
no more green fingers 79
the incremental stages of grief.....80
iomante 81

we ate berries 83

maybe he's born with it; maybe it's communion wafers 85

conversations in the lavender hedge 86

next time we will not build ships.87

imperfect reflections/kusurlu yansımalar..88

dear Santa for Christmas I would like..89

Hireath 90

we all turn our eyes to heaven 91

don't fly 96

a comedy to those who think 97

Christopher says 98

I'm sick of you always saying "I" like you matter 100

kenneth williams obituary song102

trans nun speaks 103

The Wanderer's Song....................105

iomante 2 106

airport boy......................................107

Mutual growth................................108

you can't always get what i want 109

immigrant arts 111

narcissus writes a love song.......113

final summer....................................114

weightwatchers 115

grief is stored in the poem 117
ancestors..118
geology...120
unsick..121
good times are coming soon.......122
water cycle...123
runnymede 129
the art...131

Introduction

These collected works cover an extremely difficult period filled with personal hurdles and changes, as well as what feel like global ones. Sometimes that has been expressed in verse; just as often it has resulted in not writing for many months.

There's been a lean away from rhymed, rhythmic poetry and towards greater urgency and rawness in this collection; likewise, the content has changed. There are far fewer love poems, and more political and geographic ones. Introspection remains, but is joined by a higher number of epitaphs/eulogies, as a number of deaths at closer emotional remove took up a great deal of mental space.

Place, loss, and the past move to the forefront in this collection, most of all.

Poems

do nothing

The first night, they burn your house down;
They won't let you put the fire out.

When the flames are gone, the people of the town
Gather to sigh as you rave and you shout.

"Can't you just be grateful you're not on fire any more?
Can't you just be grateful that you're not dead?"

When lightning strikes the old oak tree you make sure
Not to mention how fire spreads.

last quarter before the equinox

i came from the wild places
(i came from the sun)
& i am cold & i am burning
my body is a flame in the night
but the dark is all-encompassing
(but when the time is right)
i came from the wild places
& i am old & i am fearless
my body is a terror in the night
and yes the dark is everywhere
(but when the time is right)
i will flame into being like the dawn
i will make my own light.

Derek Des Anges

bath salts

someday i think i shall synthesise sunlight into
my bathwater
and with every glittering handful pour gold
across my body
perhaps it will retain its heat and incinerate me
to swift bones
a blackened silhouette a tree in winter
dissolving like an outline
into the greedy mouth of a rising sun
perhaps it will only blind me with luminescence
until i am consumed
by the tepid waters of midday upon the surface
of this freshwater ocean
this tiny pond that stands in for the waters of
the atlantic at falmouth
in some hitherto unseen tuke painting dangling
in the attic
of a lucky owner: four beautiful boys lounging
in the shallow water
as the light dances off the wavelets and back
into their faces
turning them into momentary angels
perhaps if i get the concentration just right by
some subtle alchemy
my philosopher's stone bathroom will transform
me into those laughing boys

stretched out forever on a summer's day a
century ago
no time like their present no future bombs and
war-weary body count
only companionship and endless summer in the
tangle of the limbs
naked on the black rocks

Derek Des Anges

urban planning & the enclosure act

When you build a fence the neighbours don't
Pop Around any more;
the dogs don't run across your lawn and leave
turds
dotted around the fish pond, and children don't
run screaming
around and over your flowerbeds, when you
build a fence
the garden is defined as a garden, it is no longer
whatever the casual wanderer-in makes of it.

Building a fence on common land makes it
private;
private land has rules and permissions; at first
they are
incredulous—it's always been public before
What do you mean I can't sit here
This is where I've always walked
Then they're angry, of course, and at last
No one will visit at all.

We hate what you've done with the place

The gate remains locked. A lifetime as a park
means there's no grasp on how to send out

RSVPs
No understanding of the way to tie party
balloons to the railing
To indicate your willingness to be seen;
here there's just a fence, and a bench
that no one will ever sit on again.

Inside the walls an untrampled bed throws up
the most
brilliant and iridescent blossoms it has ever
produced;
enjoyed in silence, and alone.

We hate what you've done with the place
Most of all
We hate that *you've* done it.

Fresh stigmata

This old stupid ache is not dead.
I thought I had lost it; killed it, rather-
I thought that I was cured of the melancholy
and the sympathy, that I had not filled
but blocked off the empty place
reflected in your words.

Oh, foolish of me, to think the ache gone,
the malaise somehow treated as if sleep
killed wakefulness, as if food killed hunger,
as if water killed thirst, instead of merely
delaying it; the old ache will not be erased.

I thought it was gone, the glorious sorrow
which rises up in me to join a great chorus
of similar lonely songs. I thought by being more
alone
I could not be persuaded; that an island sunk
was a promontory rescinded. I thought,
if I clamour, bell-like, with my tongue
the heart will not beat so.

I was wrong.

Oh God,
We have sung this song throughout history,

And I have heard your echoes in a thousand voices,
Seen my words in another's hand;
Even in isolation we have a brotherhood
Oh God help me revive this aching,
so I might understand—

I thought it was gone, I thought it was drowned,
that the face in the mirror was mine.
That by lip service solely I'd rewrite my own history,
Freed from the shackles of time and tide and weary complicity
In a masquerade I did not consent to...
Oh love forgive me,
I've found my own country,
And I swear that I never meant to.

In the 1800s I hear voices, shaping the sorrow we share—
They all know the curtain withdrawing
Or a camera's focus first found
As they look back over the centuries
To find their own footsteps abound; we are reaching
back through the history of silence, chanting each other's names.
One day I suppose I must be remembered,
And my words will bring the same—

The old ache which can never be murdered
Or cauterized out of the heart
Whose loneliness only grows greater for every
tongue whose story it imparts—the old ache
who knows we are looking and longing
for something that can never be...

Oh God you can hear I've surrendered;
somehow *I* became *we*.

What we leave behind

(for Emma W.)

Ozymandian feet and Christ's mangled
requirements
are not the sole legacy of lives lived,
Nor are we only the thousand new beginnings
our component stardust eventually witnesses,
washed up into this organism or that edifice.
Among the tangled cords of your neurons
(Say heart-strings, if you wish)
I have woven a nest of memories—
In this cocoon I am ageless and immortal,
the time-travelling shadow of every second
we have conversed.

I gain new births with each rehearsal.
My legacy is at your command,
It writhes upon your tongue, retold within
your art. In the tidal pool of your mind,
All I have been—
My fractal complexities -
Will be smoothed into meaning
At last I can be harsh when you need an enemy,
And kind when you long for a friend.

With my transition from maker to memory
My life *in* you begins
As life *with* you ends.

it was summer

(for Kasper)

wherever you go
the sun will never set now;
how does such a happy thought
always end in tears?

Derek Des Anges

two languages

(for Kasper)

It is not just exactitude or nuance
That is lost in routine translation:
Between one tongue and the next
we lose culture, lifetimes of context -
the linguistics need not differ,
only the lives. Can we ever,
truly
know someone?

A world of experience underpins
the assumed geography of the shared tongue,
a world of moments we think
are pinpricks of unity, binding us
across our many differences;
knitting us together
over our several separate scars.

When a last speaker dies, the world
of histories dies with them.
No record can ever do justice
to the highway of heart to lips;
only shadows of technicalities revive
the shallow ghost of their words.

So we cannot know the precise chill of first,

crisp snowfall,
its implications of rebirth-to-come,
the unending cycle—
We are immune to the notion, then of
the *fatness* of grief—
The way it hungers, and cannot be filled;
The pairing, inevitable to some, of transience
with eternity—
As a fallen blossom spinning forever in a
second
In the dark, cold waters of the mountain melt-
stream.

It has all been said before
But we could not hear it.

The candle burns brief and bright—
We are short lives, enclosed by night,
the moments fleeting, the tongue repeating
what words alone cannot make right.

In translation between our minds a thousand
thoughts
Go lost in misunderstanding:
Each code-switch sheds like skin cells
its load of forgotten meaning.
Where do they go, these unclaimed
communications,

Where do the words that never found an ear flee
to?

The dark of the unknown choruses
Unheard and uncomprehended
Somewhere in the hinterland of knowing
What was heard, and what was intended.

Will your name was up on those same shores
When all those who spoke it are gone,
when there is nothing left of the battle
we waged on our mortal barriers—?
Do not expect our silence
To reverberate in the black that enfolds
The guttering fire of each short life;
We are imprisoned in our own light,
broadcasting across the tideless seas of nothing.

But between the stars our sad songs still travel
Slow as starlight and still as explosions
To the unseen beach on which these
Long-running radio waves must break.

Here we'll lay the froth and foam of language
The undercurrents long-forgotten
In the frozen waters, with your name;
The flower in the winter stream, the steam of
morning breath in cold air, and the scream—

The wordless scream
Of a too-short heartbeat in the all-encroaching
black.

The word is "goodbye";
the kind you can't take back.

safe house

we all die valiant, save the cowards
who fled before the fight broke out;
we all die valiant, save the women
who beg, and weep, and curse, and shout;
says the policeman in his armour on the street
where the conflict turns grim and gritty.

we all die young, save the generals
who direct from the rear;
we all die young, save the leaders
who are not here;
says the soldier in the last battalion
to fall before the proud greeks.

we all die too soon, save those
who wish we had died before this begun;
we all die too soon, save those
who die in innocence, eternally young;
says the child in the boat in the last wave
to wash up before the drowning city.

we all die alone, save the shadows
vaporised in the physics-defying inferno;
we all die alone, save the craters
laid bare for generations, where nothing grows;

whispers the wind above the fields
where no man's voice speaks.

Derek Des Anges

the last runner

We found him floating
Somewhere just outside the Oort Cloud
The size of a baseball
The shape of an egg
The information contained within
Could be priceless.

He was gold and scrolled
And dented and old;
the lab called him Bob,
because he had, in gravity.
The name stuck

You're not meant to gender a robot.

Bob took forty-eight weeks
To unlock; forty-eight calendar weeks
of unceasing probing, of round-the-clock
fiddling and testing
And waxing and waning public interest.

We were so grateful when he turned out
To speak in machine code;
No one would have coped
With the motherlode of mental readjustment
Of taking in whole new states,

of quantum computing,
of tri-optic coding.

Secretly the engineers were
a little disappointed;
we could have learnt a lot from those things.

It still took another year
To translate his communications
But Bob was patient.

He'd been out there a while.

When we could at last speak,
Civilisation to alien nation—
When we could turn our questions
To his one laser eye,
When we turned to face him,
The whole world was watching...
The whole world was waiting.

Bob said: "They want me to tell you hello."

A spark to the imagination;
Oh God, oh god, the celebration—
The news feeds, timeliness filled
With giddy adulation for every step
That brought us to this exchange!

Bob said: "They have been searching for a long time
For anything else out there with a mind."

A world that had waited, as we had
For someone to answer—had reached out
their hands to the stars and cried
tell us we are not alone.

A million scriptwriters poised to create
A poignant montage of our first ships—
How would we get to meet them?
What would we do to greet them?

We asked him how long ago
He began his voyage
To this solar system of ours.

His answer took calculation
And when the figure came
It fried the imagination.

We asked with bated breath,
"Are they still waiting?"
After all, we had to know.

Bob said: "They ceased transmission
Eight million years ago."

old world genealogy

All those who had the money or means
and felt oppressed by the old regimes
fled these shores for a life better paid.

While the venal, rich and corrupt
or those who keep their heads ducked
are the children of them that stayed.

only you can prevent

my lineage is a forest fire
it starts and ends with me
oh sure there are sparks;
every conflagration has a beginning
and there will be scorch-marks
because no fire leaves the world
unscathed; but believe me
when i die
no part of my "family"
no drop of my "blood"
no word of my "culture"
will i save.

woodsman

i would like to say
i was hungry
that i watched
that i waited

i would like to say
i was a shadow
that i followed
that i came

i would like to say
i was constant
like a heartbeat
like a cancer

i would like to say
i persisted
like failure
like terror

but you know
i was unremarkable
a blister
a figment

and i was impatient
and i was blinded
and i was stubborn
i was a rock in the stream
and you cured yourself of me
you succeeded
you were braver

i was sated
and you were free.

tourist tout

The song unfurls each night
from uncorrupted lungs;
the casual roar of minicab fire,
friendly and unfriendly horns,
and the percussion section of impatient cyclists'
bells
{*get off the cycle path*}
purgatory sounds like announcements
of a good service running on all
other lines, while the minutes tick past
and the LED screen tells you
to listen for further, further, further—
the catechism unfinished,
but a decade of habit sings
the remainder in your head;
this too is magic, the ugly realisation
that despite map, compass, best intentions,
Red Bull, stars, and hope
you have come in a full circle
and here is the spire of St Botolph's of Aldgate,
repeating like a kebab hiccup.

The tide is eternal. The smells, seasonal.
Hot bins give way to hot nuts.
The street vendors change hats.
Omnipresent diesel buses overlay leaf mould,

unchanging ganj perfumes blocked drains,
corps-y river, dead pigeons, sweaty buses.
Onions cooking, tinted-windowed beetles
crawl through Knightsbridge
towards bright blue lights on every tree.
We are polluted not by the light,
nor by the darkness;
the river sleeps between her heaving banks,
the river androgyne (born a man, growing
a woman, fed with garbage, children,
wishes, coins, spit, shit, vomit, and
veneration), the river holy,
the river wholly incarnate,
the river elemental and eternal,
the river ephemeral.

There is sediment but not sentiment,
no palatial parade goes uncluttered,
a Victorian drawing room of a city,
alive and teeming, filthy and gleaming,
we build and we burn and we build and we
devour and we build
and we build and we build—
connected like neurons, connected like sleep
and death.

No one cares—that is our curse and our guiding
principle
(our principal is capital, filthy lucre, love,

our currency is in the currents,
which brought us garlic to the hythe
and tobacco to the dock and money,
money from the misery of men,
money from Asante's slaves,
money from cotton,
money from India's starvation,
money from more cotton,
money black with miners' tears,
money, money, money, oh—!)

We build, and we devour //

By the river towers fire light,
shine the burning touch of the dying sun,
shine like earth-bound stars.

Who
who
who speaks to you in our exported tongue
{*we had to re-mortgage the house to get*
Tamara into a good school, it's outrageous}
{*don't give out like you weren't up for it*}
{*mate, I said, mate, I said, you don't know*
fucking nothing}
{*here we have a sorry sight, a sorry sight*
indeed}
{*listen mate—*}
who sings to you in every last corrupted lung

by the banks of the river holy
we build and we burn
we build and we devour
we build and we build
by the river holy
holy and devour
we build

{lon'den}

the penitent wife

they called him a tyrant, after,
and i was
"poor little fool";
but at the end of each week
on our knees
they still tell us
love is terror
and to submit to suffering
is to be cleansed
how was i to know
which suffering was holy
and which was profane
how was i to know
which raised hand
to kiss?

Derek Des Anges

appetites

they say death is always greedy
but we know she is abstemious
it is life that teaches us to hunger—

you call down the moon from his orbit
ask for his cloak, eat his rabbit,
wrap up the night in pastry,
choke on the crumbs

—stay greedy
hunger always for the next meal,
friend,
breath,
heartbeat,
beep.

beep.

stay greedy and ask for the moon
demand the sun
fight for another heartbeat,

[*beep*]

they know to live is to hunger;
we hunger for your hunger

we are greedy for your greed—

do not starve any longer
awake, with us
and feed-

beep. *beep*.

awake with us
my greedy friend,
before the moon rises again:
partake, partake
oh hungry life

do not abstain.

Baphomet

i am a monster
a fucking monster
in name and thought
in word and in deed
i am a fucking monster
it permeates everything about me
a god-destroying monster
indeed

there is no justification
in this declaration
i am a goddamn monster
in thought and word and deed
it is an explanation
the only one you need
i am a fucking monster
and that is nothing but the truth
but this is just an explanation

it is not my excuse.

The Map-Maker's Lament on Losing His Daughter

There is no chart for death,
only questions.

Who set us upon this endless course,
where even the seabirds have abandoned
their accompaniment of mourning cries?
What has made carrion-fish of us?
Where shall we turn our sails,
now that the land of childhood
has become impassable with storms?

When can we go home?

And why are we so desperate to feed upon
the suffering of others, so hungry
for connection, so claw-handed in our desire
for jagged words to pierce away the platitudes
and wreck a bark of honesty upon the rocks
of our submerged grief?

Must we all be always navigating the shores
of missing souls alone? Oh how we scan
the horizons of loneliness,
begging for the fleet to appear and stage
a daring vigil.

No rescue needed. Only light the lanterns,
run up the colours, and sound the cannon:
we are not alone in the dark.

Migrate or Die

Don't wait up, I'm not coming home;
the melancholy season has called me away,
and this grey-winged bird has finally flown.

The seasons claimed me for their own,
stripping my sighs to silence day by day.
Don't wait up, I'm not coming home—

my final message on your unanswered phone
sounds callous, but I've nothing more to say,
and this grey-winged bird has finally flown.

So I've slipped the leash, run off alone,
and though trials follow, come what may:
Don't wait up, I'm not coming home.

What made a racing pigeon of this standing
stone?
The roost's too cold for me to stay,
and this grey-winged bird has finally flown.

But seek me out when you too have grown
tired of the arctic chill of the safest way.
Don't wait up, I'm not coming home;
and this grey-winged bird has finally flown.

Derek Des Anges

Hard Bastard

Qualities that keep the onlooker's eyes' bright:
a vitreous lustre, strong cleavage, a system of
elegant rotation—
Depths that sparkle in the light.

We're waiting for chaos, gearing for the fight,
as soft words break to sudden provocation—
qualities that keep the onlooker's eyes' bright,

when looking for a bird that won't take flight.
A diamond geezer, that's the proclamation,
depths that sparkle in the light,

Like a fire consuming almost all it might
in a single violent conflagration—
qualities that keep the onlooker's eyes' bright.

I'm not the one. My aggression's shite.
The surface flares alone wow the nation,
depths that sparkle in the light

sadly lacking. Dull earth, not iron pyrite:
I'll not be fools' gold in your estimation.
Qualities that keep the onlooker's eyes' bright:
depths that sparkle in the light.

forgotten feelings

he touches you and for a moment you wish
that his skin would stain yours like the mark
of ink against a fresh sheet of paper
or the scorch of bleach upon black velvet cloth;
you feel as tainted by it
as burned by it;
and you wish you could wipe off
the tell-tale thump and flutter
inside your heavy heart
the swoop and swirl of secret longing
somewhere in your stomach
that screams as his hand departs;
do it again
do it again
whatever you meant to start
finish it

Derek Des Anges

that martha stewart feeling

i want to go home
wherever that is
however far back that is
somewhere i can start again;
to take my hand off the guard rail
and walk upstairs marvelling at the texture of
the carpet;
to feel safe when i close the door
to want to be shut in with these people,
where i am not always making plans for escape
yearning for some intruder
to open the door
and whisk the world out of shape.

i want to go home
whatever that is
whenever that is
where the darkness can always be illuminated
and warmth is not a sin
and hunger exists to be sated
and worth is not debated
on whether or not your interlocutor is tired;
to touch familiarity
and not be repelled by it
or expelled by it
on a whim.

i want to know home
is people and not a place,
like they tell you
in the movies;
i want to know home
as a certainty,
a rock
in the sea of change;
i want to see faces that resemble
the ones that i can abide;
i want to walk weary to the door of a new
sanctuary
and finally feel safer
inside.

identity cards and the body politic

you don't write "trans poetry"
you just write this stuff about
birds and cities and dirt and
anyone could write that it's not
unique it's not saleable it's not "trans";
if you're going to have this gender agenda
you have to talk about your
body
you have to strip down
to your bones
and show us your
guts
and your
body
and your cunt
and your sadness
and your alienation
satisfy our curiosity
satisfy our voyeurism
satisfy our needs our desires
show us your pink bits
perform every kind
of strip tease
if you don't fit in with these
demands on your language
why should we care;

your truths are narrow
you are your body
just a body
not a body of work;
only one type of person
gets to be
an unseen commentator
on the nature of nature
there's only one kind of experience
that's allowed to be universal
and it's
not
yours

my sincere and open-handed apology
but every word that's flowed
from these trans paws
these little gay hands
is tinted and tainted with
what's hinted and painted in the hue
of my own language
that has evolved on the tongue
of a trans
in the head
of a trans
of a man
who didn't begin
as the universal experience
that is no such thing;

it isn't my fault you're impounded
by your own unbounded universality
and too wide-eyed blinded to notice
that every bird and dirt and city
every urban pastoral and stellar panegyric
every burdensome longing and
prosodic elegy for the departed friends
is composed through the filter
that's printed with an identity
i cannot *not* claim…

my own universe
my own me.

can you feel me dancing

heroic is the man who can dance
with a rifle strapped to his back
heroic is the woman who can dance
with her child dying in her arms
heroic is the child who can dance
with the dogs of hunger snapping at his belly
the dance looks like trudging
and the obstacles are many
but we advance
oh yes we dance.

and damned are the stiff-backed
the stiff-lipped and the sitters
the 'i don't feel like dancing'
the 'i'm more of a singer's
and the quitters
and damned are those who let
their partners drop behind them
and damned are those who don't dance on the spot
while the slowest fly to find them
but rush on like runners
without a backward glance
we may be carrying warheads
but my god
we will dance.

perhaps you can only sway a little
it's enough, you understand
to nod your head or twitch your eyes
and if you can, to clap your hands;
spin your wheelchair, clear a space
the greatest dance is enthusiasm
persistence the only grace;
the only enemies are the watchers
the judgement from the stands
we will not break our pace and turn to face
the respect that they demand
just stir our bodies ever-on
to the place the sun commands:
you may kill us one by one
but by the devil
we will dance.

we don't all get back up
the tide recedes, the crowd proceeds
once again we find our feet
but each new disaster paves the world faster
with bones that grow as thick as reeds
our river beds are swollen with shoes
the wrists we couldn't grasp
their names are slipping away at last
we don't all get back up
but while we can, we *dance*.

memory is rewritten, not recalled

i would like to rewind
and remind the lonely child
on the steps of countless buildings
in a thousand cold carparks
that he contains the kernel
of everything he will become
and thus ingest that knowledge
as a wholesome meal
to carry me through
to my own adulthood

but the carparks of the past
are not the place for imparting wisdom
and what he needed in him
i still cannot give
the adolescent on the gurney
dripping saline into soft tissues
cannot be reasoned with
i still have no solid reason
to offer him to live

i know my own reflection
well enough to recall
that i would never have listened
and besides those shadows

don't feel like the same person
at all.

cypress path

down
the darkened avenue
hooded leaning trees
guard the night
in naval hues
and through
the oppressive blues
where even stars
are shy of shining
he screams
a path of fire
my golden boy
burning
the moths from
this final night
drawing me in
as helpless as them
he never slows
i cannot keep pace
and the ink streak shadows
grow deeper
after he fades.

Derek Des Anges

give up your love poems

there's no fleshly thing
that can satisfy me now
unless it comes in multitudes
and radiates its affection
like an incandescent dust cloud;

i first came for the agony
i'm staying for the dance

only void and stars below
and the scorched winds above
don't talk to me about beauty
don't sing to me of love
my feet don't move for emotions.

i've come for the light
i'm staying for the dance

they said my body was a mistake
and my words were humiliation;
you can't see i'm no static body,
no permanent creation to be beheld;
i'm all electron and no shell

i've come for the dance
i'm staying for the dance

a movement in the heavens
not a shitty shadow self.

Derek Des Anges

too realistic for poetry

I've become too realistic for poetry
Fell out of love with falling in love;
It used to make me feel alive
But now I only feel guilty.

There's no "you" to turn my well-worded
suffering to.

All this lyricism turned to heavy prose
A brief paean to the sunrise swallowed
To the same place all exultation goes
I don't want to share my joys and sighs
Secrets are the better for being forgotten
not kept.

Sleep only wears a hole in my resolve
And though I black out each dawn
It's been a year since I last wept;
Too many things to drink about
Too little time to unfurl in
Every nascent shoot of spoken word
Must be stifled like a changeling child.

I am trying to build a city in this wilderness
And all my bricks are rotten
My secrets still are kept

But my system of speaking is forgotten;
grew out of growing verbose
Now all my pacing's morose
And the release no longer comes.

I traded a stable pair of feet
for my heart and tongue.

Derek Des Anges

more life

i am afraid i did not keep up
my end of the bargain;
should have kept a finger on
the buttons of your cuff
at the very least;
the scree slope was as rough
as the cliff face you'd scrambled up
and maybe i thought there were
so many hands all reaching
that it would be enough
you'd always been so competent
at cording your own rope
from strands of blackened despair
perhaps i gave up giving up hope;
i am afraid i did not listen
to every whisper on the wind
every footstep on the boards
before you began to fall
before your fingers missed their mark
and now i remember too late
to thrust my hand back into the dark
and find it empty
when i pull it back.

hillier's remnants

my late grandfather kept several greenhouses
being not so much a keen gardener
as a man obsessively addicted to the nurture of
plants
the identification of plants
the cataloguing of plants
and the photographing of plants
nor was he content to extend non-judgmental
affection
to every growing thing;
his ire for dandelions and dogs
knew no bounds; he'd have happily taken
an air rifle to a cat were it allowed.

in all my fondest memories the light is low,
the rosy air of early summer sunsets
just topping a high hedge of cypress trees
to kiss the six different varieties of apples
just beginning to blossom;
the world smells of potting compost
and broken terracotta,
with tiny green seedlings scrabbling
for the sun beneath their window-pane homes
and the rough flint gravel crunches
like the teeth of giants
and there is a thrush yelling out

a territorial boundary
and my grandfather
has just called someone
a bugger.

in later years the garden house smelt of mould
and the carpets set my teeth on edge;
i was relegated to lonely darkness
when the whole family gathered to celebrate
some forgotten christianity or other.
i buried myself in books
and the town shrank until there was only
silence and decay,
cat shit in the paved alleyway
and a mumbling, repeated lecture
about the same slides we had all seen before—
the universe was filled with rain
and possibilities disappeared
as each mysterious painted door in a garden
wall
was resolved into leading
only to places i couldn't go.

though the light will never look that way again
and even the vastest english gardens
are tiny in their familiarity
some things remain constant;
now that the cats are safe from curses
i have no one to ask for classification

of every sprout and shrub
it must be enough to have a memory
and to know that whatever else i may be
i am stalwartly and steadfastly
a bugger.

Derek Des Anges

What goes around

Perhaps it is time we asked a new question:
Not "why do we fight?"
But "how do we stop?"
It has been so long
Even the flowers are born red
And all our laughter sounds
like falling bullets.

There's no escaping the maze without a lamp

Before the fall there was a cliff edge
looming huge in my eyes; I could see that
I was not born to swim but to fly—
there was a sun above and wings on my back
and I, I was a fragile feathered thing
beautiful as gold, made to burn and die;
Now in stately calm contorted waters
my broken barely-singed body has to lie—
I was not built to outrun fate
so please, father, tell me why
The cliff edge recedes and leaves me deep
where nothing but weeping sustains me
I was not born to swim
I was born to fly
And it was you who launched me
full-fledged into the cloudless sky
Now storms have stolen my birth right
and here am I
an albatross who cannot wander,
a sun-worshipper six fathoms under
A broken-hearted boy with no reason to cry;
I cannot steer by stars alone
and night's about to slip straight by—
Let me rise once more with the sun
Let me find one more worth looking on

Derek Des Anges

I was not born to drown
I am steam and I will rise
I was not born to stay down
I tell you I was made to fly.

recruitment drive

looking for one last crusade
one bright and brilliant shining godhead
to lay down my life to follow;
i have arms i've spent a lifetime forging
please give me the banner
behind which to march;
listen i've been preparing
a clutch of love poems that would break your
heart
all i'm asking for is someone to yearn after
for more than a moment
let me start afresh
with this long-legged lovesickness
i've somehow cured myself from;
what's a poet to do with security
what's a poet to do with mundanity
what's a poet to do with the grudging admission
that no one is much of a saint?
there's no hunger in my heart
no fire in my veins
and all the world offers me
is more of the same.

Derek Des Anges

far from damascus (attempt 1)

the wind has ripped my breath
across cities and desert lands
from green prisons to the clean
open sterility traversed
by singing sun-scorched bands
of men whose eyes are undaunted
by the constraint of sunday rest;
turning my prayer to the sands
to the particles of silica
a thousand flies dead upon the floor
of some vanished ocean;
my silhouette falls, i understand,
beneath these robust sea-skies
upon a tide of dry white stars;
hear this hoarse plea to the god
i'm not on good terms with
as i raise each scoured hand;
my lord, make me anything
anything
anything other
than that which i am

unWanton

the loneliness will drive you mad
(i want it to, i want it to)
my body is the house you pass
a shadow of a former habitation
and shaking your head, murmur
someone should live there;
never stopping to check for a key.
solitude becomes you, they said,
(i have become the silence
that i howled into for years)
my body is the unmarked road
only familiar travellers turn down,
their route already mapped.
this mirror is transparent
and i can see you refusing
to look in; this ugliness is caustic
but it is mine to live with.
the loneliness will drive you mad
(it has, it has)
the cure is in your hands
but you'd rather be the one
who keeps to paved roads
and inhabited neighbourhoods;
who wants an overgrown track
a derelict house
soiled goods?

Derek Des Anges

Like Father, Not Sun

In wild disarray I face the eternal fire,
Drenched in waxen sweat and love's bright
tears,
And still the flickering flames cry, "Go higher."

Our situation once seemed deathly dire,
Trapped in pater-built prison for years,
But still the flickering flames cried, "Go
higher."

And wings were fashioned without nail or wire,
By my self-same father, diverting fate's gears,
So in wild disarray I might face the eternal
fire—

Though he bid me without cease, did not tire
Of telling me I should not rise: he spoke his
fears,
And still the flickering flames cried, "Go
higher."

It is parents' way to gripe and grouse 'til they
expire
That sons should be like their own yesteryears,
And not in wild disarray face the eternal fire.

Please, my sainted father, I say, bend your ears
Listen how the rising golden god sends his cheers
As in wild disarray I face the eternal fire
And *still* his flickering flames cry, "Icarus, go higher."

Derek Des Anges

silhouettes in an east london flat

they are so gentle with each other
you can tell they don't hate each other at all;

when we are in the crystallising period of love
still growing our mineral skeletons
we exchange pieces of ourselves
stories and memories, words and habits
to create a structure that is two people
sometimes it lasts

other times the weather that drives people
together
eventually pulls them apart
hands them umbrellas
and launches them back into the storm

romance should not be derived from pressure
cookers
i wonder if there is anything to love in me;
the people who profess to find it
stab at shadows and howl at echoes
replicas of their own reflections
set up to dazzle them into compliance

there is no art in this science of serial seduction

there is a deformity of the eye
that allows you to see only the mundanity
the wretchedness and ugly reality;
shit-tinted shades
showing off the grim compromise
the worms at the core
and the lies

when we demolish the fabric of a certainty
it unravels between our fingers
leaving them stained and scratched
and it burns out the ladders
leaving no way back

they are gentle with each other
and i have forgotten how to stay my hand
or blunt my tongue
there is only antarctica to freeze my course
time to slow down
until i can hurt no one

they are gentle with each other
and i should have learned that trick
when i was young.

Derek Des Anges

temporal lobe seizure

Begin at the beginning
if you know where that is;
a leaf becomes leaf not bud
at a specific point in the fourth dimension
that is time
and in that other dimensions after
is an U N F U R L I N G
time coaxes breadth depth and width
into chemical expansion
and bud becomes leaf
an arbitrary conception
but a functional one
as bud cannot photosynthesise
cannot farm the photons
descending millions of miles
another meaningless measure
to strike the surface of this
discrete unit of organism and
perform evolution's rank alchemy
making energy from energy
it is utilitarian romance
leaf becomes leaf when it can do the job of a
leaf
but in our clinging lingering ontology
leaf does not cease to be leaf
when it is brown and incapable

nor when it is severed and separate from
its purpose the plant or tree
another purely conceptual distinction
the leaf
is still leaf until it decoheres
and is invisible and consumed
we say
and we say
the same of people
the leaf fidgets in turbulence
and falls on the wind
and is dispersed
it is coalesced in the body of the tree
from nutrients
made in part in other leaves
from the sun's streaming light
if you follow a leaf forever
how many other things is it
where does it come from
where does it go
is it more leaf than tree
more tree than sun
more sun than bugs
or birds or mould
are these all just stages of nameless
eternal life of individual particles
do these molecules these atoms
do they remember everything they have been
if you look at the motions of matter

there must be nets
and webs
and patterns
the atoms composing sap
circulating
and breaking out inside animal bellies
moving into their blood their bones
you could see the entire story of existence
written in subatomic wriggles
a hieroglyphic language of everything
the map is the territory
with the right kind of eyes

greenery from blackening

in western america
and australia there are trees
whose lives are so often scarred
by serious conflagration
that they require an inferno
simply to germinate;
see how easy it is
for survivors to turn
what they have suffered
into their necessity.

the carpathian mountains once held
mythical avians whose millennia of life
terminated in inferno
on pyres deliberately constructed
to house their infant selves
in the aftermath of the heat;
see how easy it is
to be prepared only
for the worst to come.

we who have placed our children in boats
close to sinking, and waded out
into uncertain waters;
we who have crowded freezing
at harshly-guarded borders

Derek Des Anges

peppered with shot for the chance
to bleed in a hospital bed
instead of the naked street;
we who have yet to untangle
the touch of love
from the terror of a raised fist
cannot afford to be patient
but can teach every luckier man
what it is to become fireproof.

in our scars may you learn
the truth behind propaganda
and distorting lightbulb flashes;
may you never have to know
what was burned,
and what arose from the ashes.

valley of long-forgotten kings

i will learn the stars from you
and the names of all your kings
in return i give you the descent of man
from single-celled life
and the story of every white-worm scar
that has healed upon my hands;
give me the lives of your lovers
who were cast off like skins before me
i will be the next god of your idolatry
if you will only adore me;
but teach me everything you know
and i will fill you with wisdom
i know you fear the conditions of love
well my love
this is one.

credon't

"I"
is a delusion
caused by too many reflections
the only sickness worse
is "we".

message from the gods

you are a circle
complete in and of yourself
you don't need
anybody else

but embrace another
and you both gain
two circles after all
begin a chain

it can connect you
though i will not lie
a chain can bind
a chain can tie

it is your choice
to reach or to stand
to remain alone
or clasp a hand

you are a circle
complete in yourself
you do not need
only want
somebody else

i have no time for romance

i held you in my hands
thinking of the difference
between who kisses
and who is kissed
and why it matters so much
who started this.

global

well, there's the question:
is it better to separate ourselves entirely
and live free of each other
never interacting
or to remain in a state of
continual tension
until someone forgives
and healing can begin;
my heart says run
but it always says run
it was born wearing cleats
a passport in the aorta
no forwarding address
and two thousand aliases
what if you want to absolve me;
what if i don't want you to
a grudge is the only way
i can pay for my ticket
to a place where i no longer have to be
the person i was.

keep hating.

no more green fingers

love fled before me like grass before the scythe
and not the draining of the tide:
it is gone, felled and scattered
transformed and digested.
it will be several seasons before
anything can grow here again;
perhaps i am barren ground now,
all my growing given up,
the recycled love given over to feed
someone else's garden.

the incremental stages of grief

cleaning out old birthday cards i find her name;
the image is non-descript—ugly, even—
and the message is banal, or at least plain;
so i'd have no qualm about tossing it out—
but i know i'll never get a card from her again.

Derek Des Anges

iomante

it begins with communion
(we should always eat our gods)
when tongue tip touches flesh
transformed by some salival magic
from the dusty bones of wheat
into leaving bleeding meat

it begins with hunger
(we should always eat our gods)
the kind that will not be satisfied
with ripe berries and fat cakes
or the wiped-up remnants of fried
breakfasts and wafer-cone flakes

it begins with necessity
(we should always eat our gods)
when the harvest doesn't come
and the baby is still-born
and the winter is too long
when there's a thought that doesn't
belong

it begins with love
(we should always eat our gods)
with your head on their thigh
wondering how it would taste

to just turn
and not hold back

it begins with decay
when our gods
return the favour

and we find that in the final reckoning
death has the finest flavour

Derek Des Anges

we ate berries

oh summer sun you wake the sleeper
wedged safe beneath the black coastal rock;
you drag from the cave the slick-hide waiter
who flashes quicksilver swift across the water
the glass-clear water at bathers' ankles
you dredge up, oh summer sun,
the fires in the long dry grass
who stilled and did not stir
the whole winter past; you give them
sparks, you make the landscape
scorched charcoal stark, you make
desolation into a fine art.

oh summer sun you rouse me
from the grey to the green
from the brown trails to the golden
as the leaves spring forth to greet
the passing of the unseen;
the nape of the neck of summer
the thick-haired belly of the summer
the fitful sleep of the summer
who holds off his hand until daylight
and leaves the torrid nights for waking.

oh summer sun you send me
high-spirited, light-healed across the moor

down the cliffs to the shouting gulls
to the broken ships and steep sandbanks
to my home once more; you send me
a hundred forgotten moments
like hovering flies to taunt
with all the things my skin has seen
and remind me with too-hot kisses
what you used to mean.

oh summer sun i missed you
and will miss you again
i'll return again some older
a little greyer
still your friend.

Derek Des Anges

maybe he's born with it; maybe it's communion wafers

heaven is perhaps just when we start again
at the beginning
a different beginning
and this time you're there
and you say
i'm sorry i took so long
the time wasn't right
and this time it will be okay

so i'll try to remember
when i'm staring weeks of death
squarely in their ugly faces
when my body screams
to run for safety
that pain is the price we pay
for being late
and that next time will be better

heaven is perhaps just when
i don't have to write this
when i compose nothing
when i lack nothing
when i fear nothing

conversations in the lavender hedge

here's what i want
if you're granting wishes:
i want a home
that i can return to
whenever i am tired
and need to be alone;
i want to be fed
when i am hungry
i want to be led
when i am lost
i want to be told
when i am short of love for myself
that you have enough for us both;
i want a handsome man
to kiss me when he's sober
and mean it;
and when i die, which i must
i want to go fast
and warm
and taken wholly by surprise
a good death
like a good kiss
should be something you mean.

Derek Des Anges

next time we will not build ships

Next time we will not build ships
No, we will wade out in the waters
And eyeball the horizon where the sun lives
Knowing that where the light lies
Is also where the night is born;
We will accept that time is not to be caught in
cogs and bars
But to be glimpsed in all the air kissed by a
falling leaf
To be reflected in the many tears of the dancing
stream.
We will appreciate this island for what it is:
A prison to protect the world from us
And we will listen, my love,
We will obey when our parents say
Do not cross the ocean today
—next time we will not die on the battlefield
—next time we will not to Troy
—next time we will smooth clay with our
clinging fingers
And soothe pain with our careful words
We will create, and not destroy and we will
not—
Next time
Next time... We will not build ships.

imperfect reflections/kusurlu yansımalar

bir imparatorluktan geliyorum
bir imparatorun dilinde konuşuyorum
ben bir imparator değilim
ama onun sözleri benden konuşuyor
ağzım açıkken
bir imparatorluk bir aç yaratıktır
o geçmişi yiyor
biz bir imparatorluktan önce neydik?
biz ne olacağız
tek sahip olduğum bir dil
ama dil imparatora aittir
ve ne dediğimi bilmiyorum

i come from an empire
i speak in an emperor's tongue
i am not an emperor
but his words speak out of me
when my mouth is open
an empire is a hungry beast
it eats the past
what were we before we were an empire
what will we be
all i have is a tongue
but the tongue is the emperor's
and i do not know if it is mine

Derek Des Anges

dear Santa for Christmas I would like

To be touched with a surreptitious finger
To be beckoned with a half-smile
To be the spot-lit focus of a sly sideways look
And draw a blanket of secrecy about this public
meeting

Salutations to my better self
A romance worth prolonging
And tomorrows that improve relentlessly
On each passing today

Some heart beats in delighted anticipation
A connection made and not regretted
Welcome silences, changed minds, a gallery of
beautiful and meaningless ephemera
And a hundred new beginnings.

Hireath

You tell me I'm a traitor
And I say; a blade is never used
In the place that it is made.

And whose infidelity is greater
The one who left hearth and home
Or the hearthstone that decayed?

Whatever I return as
There is no home to go back to
Now the myth was left to die;

The worst kind of Judas
Your treachery doesn't even leave me
With a kiss to remember you by.

Derek Des Anges

we all turn our eyes to heaven

How does an atheist pray?

If enlightenment is just a feeling
Made of chemicals in the brain
And cannot be trusted

If connectedness is just a feeling
Made of chemicals in the brain
And cannot be trusted,

How does an atheist pray?

If connectedness is made of chemicals in the
brain
And the chemicals (proteins) are made of
molecules
And the molecules are made of atoms
And the atoms are made of particles
Created at the birth of the universe
Like all matter, like all power

Then isn't every particle my brother
Isn't every molecule my sister
Isn't every protein my family
Isn't every part of this universe connected to
me

In the white hot heat of the beginning?

Isn't that feeling correct?
Don't we connect?

(And who will love you if there is no God to
love you?

Oh then I will love me, and I will forgive me,
and I will absolve me;
And I won't ask for worship
And I won't ask for prayers
And I won't tell the loving other people
To abandon the love of theirs)

How do atheists pray, though, if you have no
soul

If all you are is matter
Why do you matter

How do atheists pray, then, if you're empty as a
bowl?

If all I am is matter, am I different from a rock
Do I have a claim upon the space that I take up?
But there is no other matter
Like the matter I'm made of

Every single moment of my life is only mine
And every single molecule has changed over
time
And every single combination of events
Means there's nothing identical to me
In this whole firmament

If all I am is matter I am still unique
I am the only me that will ever exist

The same is true of granite
But I'm okay with this.

(And though I am unique, I am never alone:
The microbes in my body feed me
The atoms in the air sustain me
And when death comes to bleed me
My body will become
A million other things)

How do atheists endure, if you've no God to
hold you

If there is no power beside you
In the darkest moments of your life
There's no one to guide you
Through the longest night

How do atheists endure, without a spirit to

enfold you?

If the night is long and lonely, the sun still rises
If my heart is broken, one day it will not matter
If my way is lost, my feet will find another
All this suffering and horror will pass

"I" may pass with it
"I" may not survive it

But it will pass.

And when the heat of the universe is gone at
last
My particles will lie
In the sea of room-temperature nothing
With nothing to differentiate me
From the neighbours I loved
The foes I feared
The plants that I ate
And the worms that ate me

I need no gods to love me or demons to hate
me;

This will pass

Time is intemperate
Nothing lasts

This will pass.

How do atheists pray then? A little like this:

I am connected
I am unique
All this will pass
But for now

I exist.

don't fly

The soul is not a butterfly
It is a worm bored into the body
Eating through the dirt of the world
Making fertile thought from foul experience;

When poisonous pain makes a monster
Of the person you remember
And their body cracks and leaves them
Screaming and naked of their humanity
In the dark animal underbelly where all
Is physical and nothing is certain,

Do not pray for the chrysalis to peel back
And emit the soul into some unknown
salvation:

Feed the worm in your own chest.

Derek Des Anges

a comedy to those who think

nihilists must be miserable
for only in finding meaning
can we compensate for the suffering
that is our fate.

i refuse to dignify my suffering
with the application of meaning
elevate that sorry state
to something it is not.

life may be suffering
but suffering is absurd
existence is an accident
a random joke at the expense
of sentience.

i am put upon this earth
for no reason whatsoever
my consciousness is merely chance
nothing i do will change that
it does not mean i will do nothing

futility is the best joke of all
i was put upon this earth
to *laugh.*

Christopher says

Christopher says
you're a fool to think I loved you
here, let me tell you the truth
I played your lover to protect the world from
you
I knew you were the worst of us
I had to keep them safe.

Christopher says
look at yourself
I sacrificed myself to stop you
and it wasn't enough
you just wanted more of my love.

Christopher says
now I don't need you
won't heed you
a fool in braggart's clothing
what do you know of love
you only know loathing.

you say
why not just kill me
If I am that bad

Christopher takes your hand and says
you poor fool—
I have.

I'm sick of you always saying "I" like you matter

i don't love, any more
I do not want to be cured.

innocence has no age, no race, no gender
it is in deed, in thought, in word
in selflessness
in honesty
in making an effort to remember
ignorance is not innocence
& neither is inexperience

irritation is the first symptom of emotional
obsolescence;
i believe that
if i believe anything at all

it's cold and beautiful on top of the world
irrespective of whose land it is

i'm sorry i ever opened my mouth but
in the depths of space there are
innumerable mysteries we are only beginning to
unravel
& you don't care, you don't care

Derek Des Anges

i don't love, any more
i dwell in the house of awe
imagining brighter futures
& you don't figure in them at all.

kenneth williams obituary song

i don't want anyone to touch me
means so many things
[i don't want *you* to]
so many things
[i don't want *any of you people* to touch me, i'm
tired of your presumption, i'm tired of the
struggle to get away]
so many little things
[i don't want to have to explain myself]
none of them worth saying
[i don't want anyone but someone i don't know
yet to touch me]
none of them easy to explain
[i don't want to want him to touch me]
or to take back
[i don't want to enjoy it]
or to say
[i don't want to find out i could have done this
sooner]
means so many things
i don't want anyone to touch me

and i'm not reaching out first.

trans nun speaks

god does not make mistakes

it's for mortals to be incorrect
and to assume we are informed
of the content of her intent
and that we are somehow worthy
of the divine authority
of judgement

god does not make mistakes

only god knows why I was given this soul
brought into the world splintered
while others arrived whole
only god knows my purpose
only god knows my service
only god knows
why you think I deserve this

god does not make mistakes

and i am not mistaken in this:
I do not know what lesson
I was made to teach
but I will teach you compassion
with my teeth bared and my hands

filled only with prayers
I do not know
why you think you know what passed
between god and i in the dark nights
of torment

but god does not make mistakes
god makes clay
it is up to us to mould it
and to master the divine art
of forgiveness
for whatever others think
we should make of it

god made no mistake with me
she did not mismake me
she asked me to be strong enough
to make myself

a woman.

amen

Derek Des Anges

The Wanderer's Song

No land but the soles of my feet
no tongue but what holds my spit
you say all men should have a country
but I say I want none of it:

no language to hold and bind me
no bones and borders to shelter in
no faith or family to blind me
to that final battle no one wins.

You all say 'close-knit society'
like it's something all should do
and so forget that which shields
will also strangle you.

Loose weave lets me live freer
and draw more honest breath
and because I don't clutch onto life
oh strangers, *I fear no death*

iomante 2

you smile like a god
implacable and as hungry as the void
at the centre of the universe.
I can't believe in benevolence
indifference is the best bet I can see:
when I say 'a god' please have faith
I mean you look like
you could devour me

airport boy

i dream of us only in transit
we meet on an aeroplane, or a bus
our future homes are ephemeral, global
pied-à-terres in a hundred bruising cities
one foot already raised to move again
as here I sit with tap roots plunged deep
into the well of mediocrity.

i wonder was it genes that left me believing
that endless roaming is the only solution
to dissatisfaction
some family myth of Romani feet
trampling in our blood

or is there some other reason i can only see
love coming from outside a home;
that inside one
i can only see the walls of prison
or monastic cells
a place to be trapped,
and always alone.

Mutual growth

(For Maud and Fred on the occasion of their wedding)

at the place where the lake makes an elbow
there are two islets
like land-drops on the surface of the water
unremarkable but for the tangled tree that
spreads across them
or say rather trees: one on each.
spidery roots cover one micro continent
thick twisting buttresses over the other's reach
and across the channel dividing their kingdoms
two small giants lean together
a pair of individual arboreal empires embrace
one another
and become a central column
grasping for the sun
each might have striven unsupported
but they've united into one
wooden bridge across the waters
where gleeful squirrels run
and a single day grows into years
in the turning of a leaf.
such is the reward of stretching out
to take another's hand:
with a tight enough clasp we make a channel
into our own land.

Derek Des Anges

you can't always get what i want

All the umbrellas in London were laid end to
end
And they flowed down Ludgate Hill in a
hydrophobic stream
A perfect paradox like when you said to me
You'd take me anywhere I wanted to go:

I can't love a taxi service
This heart is public transit
This heart is a communist
It's for everyone all at once.

All the couriers in the Square Mile turned to a
straight line
And spelled out the lyrics to your favourite
song
As the pigeons began to sing along, and I
sighed
And you said you'd carry me, and didn't mind
the burden:

But I am certain love should be crowd-surfing
A hundred hands holding a little of my weight
You can't be a hundred people I said
But it came out too late.

All the statues in London pirouetted on their
plinths
And the wandering dispossessed grew back
their missing limbs
As you opened up your heart and told me to
come inside

But I am no taxi-taker
And I didn't hail this ride.

And all the umbrellas in London won't keep a
river from your feet
And I have love but the kind that's piecemeal,
discrete
As all the couriers go streaming screaming up
the Strand
The statues are composing an answer to your
tweet:

This heart is public transit
It's a social little Tube
My loves' workers need more unions
But with more than just you.

Derek Des Anges

immigrant arts

all you dour bastards who complain
of weeds in the cracks of paving slabs
of flowers in the crook and cranny of a wall
of the bold bright buddleia who sprouts from
the roof
with a foothold on nothing at all

you who deride these brave offerings as
"unsightly"
who sic the council upon them daily & nightly
who complain of neglect and of property prices
who think no bloom should be left to its own
devices

tell me, how does it feel to have no joy in your
heart
no sense of aesthetics, no love of the greater
nature
which flings up fragile flowers wherever it is
able—
be that location so very unstable—

how *does* it feel to be empty and scared
to reject the rewards of a nature so selflessly
shared
what gave you the desire to tear branches down

to see violence done wherever the grand wild
plays the clown

the lack of appetite for visual metaphor betrays you
this struggling bright buddleia should amaze you
the irrepressible nature that springs from the
cracks
grows like a weed but highlights your acts
it shames and dismays you to stand in the light
to see your own selfishness in another's plight

well no matter, it's your town after all
but those weeds won't give up
even if you tear down
this hateful wall

Derek Des Anges

narcissus writes a love song

i have never lived, never loved until now;
so careful with my heart, though i'd no need to be
with the disappointments of the flesh as striking
as the vacuity of souls

the void in me thirsted for more than I could see
until i looked about and there was

me

now I think I've met my match,
the mate to my soul, the string to my bow
the beat to the heart I've always had
but the face finally fits

i am so glad
to catch my own eye in the mirror.

final summer

is this what an apocalypse sounds like?
just unjust silence where once there was
a gentle and constant hum, almost unnoticed
until it is gone?

is this what it's like? flowers diminishing,
shaken only by the unseasonal breeze
as we search fruitlessly for these bodies we
barely remember;

what's to come but the inexorable damp
rising through the soles of shoes unprepared
for the running together of puddles as shores
recede
and the smell of salt that grows weaker as it
grows nearer?

is this what the end will be?
neither bang, nor whimper
just a banal wrangling over the grammar upon
our death warrant

and the unheard silence in the decaying
symphony
that was once alive with low warm hymn

weightwatchers

you're not in a fast car, and the hot boy is
absent.

The wheels on the train go *shush-clunk-
screech* and the faces are grey and bland
Like day-old paste in a bucket, and the song of
disappointed romantic hopes
Has no cigarettes, no yearning,
just *fuckitfuckitfuckit*.

the worst crime of your soul is only shoplifting;
there's no murders done here

And the wheels on the bus go *chug—chug-
chug—chug* and the seats smell of boredom
not of fear; and the men look like ashes spread
on the remains of conversation,
where hope for something better disembarked
at the last station.

you're not asking for a light, just a sense of
general direction

And the wheels on your bike are bent out of
shape by too much security,
but at least it's not stolen, and your eyes are dry

and your cheeks aren't swollen
and there's no sin of which to repent, just the
silence of boredom—
aren't you content?

the worst crime of your soul is only drifting

no body count, no forest fire, no wheels roaring
the night roads to take your desperation
higher; nothing but average as far as your eye
can reach—

and you're not asking for a light, just someone
you can miss
with the intensity that poets talk about a long-
forgotten kiss

but you're not in a fast car
and the speed limit is twenty

what's the reward in looking for love
when you've already got plenty?

Derek Des Anges

grief is stored in the poem

what a world: my grandmother was born
into one where no holocaust had yet occurred;
millions of bodies as yet unburied,
mass graves not yet dug.

my mother was born into one
where capital punishment had yet to take
its final life upon our soil
in a silhouette of a hanging on a tv screen.

and i was born to two germanies and
two towers; two tribes still going to war,
one yugoslavia
and a lovers' apocalypse in full swing.

no one will come after me,
thank god:
look at what a world i'd be leaving them to
inherit.

ancestors

I came from flesh
I was raised by fists

my place is outside
my home is the toilet cubicle I spent a
cumulative year in
the wardrobe I hid in
the lies I told

my ancestors are the hidden bodies
who begged to be buried in their clothes
my father was hanged for the touch of bearded
lips
my mother ran away to sea

my land is any city that will hold me
my home is any shroud of anonymity

you will find no blood of history on me;

well now I'm bare and the stage is wide and the
lights are bright and the words are loud on
every front page
well now you can't play blind and you must
stay dumb and I've got scars that've long
grown numb

and now I'm here with my bloody history
and all my hidden ancestors behind me
our culture moves horizontally
and my descendants will know me

well now I'm here and I've filled this page and
your time I've had and your lineage is of no
concern
your lines are all mistook

you might loathe that I come from nowhere
you might hate the roots I don't have to sever
but the likes of me will be here forever;

your lines all end in hooks

and there are no more hidden bodies
come on then if you're so desperate to see us

look.

geology.

I come from granite: unyielding and everlasting
Born in the heart of incandescent turmoil;
I ran to limestone, so changeable that
even rain wears grooves in it.
My blood runs down from slate, blue and
beautiful
And the perfect place for writing
My blood runs down from clear chalk streams,
the tool with which we write;
I come from legend, where the granite peaks
grow poetry
I come from limestone, where languages
coalesce at the mouth of a river
I have chalk and slate in my veins
But my voice is silent
And I am forgetting from whence I came.

unsick

desire when it came
used to come like a sickness
crawling too fast over infested ground
oh but I
I have been clean for years

no further questions
your honour
no further questions
mine.

good times are coming soon

no friend of mine has died by sickness
other than depression
and on days like today i forget
there's any other way to end
the court of suffering's lifelong session;
how else convince the jury that it's time to
adjourn
if you can't raise a weapon to your own flesh
how will death ever learn to take you?
if I thought there was anyone waiting in that
grey and distant land
i'd have no reason to stay my hand
so don't give me fresh hope
just give me quick goodbyes
or pass me the rope
and close your eyes.

water cycle

it rained for forty days
and ten thousand nights.

when they came, on their naked tough-soled
feet
they loved the places where the land and water
meet
and on formby shore their toes still greet the
greying air
filling with the tide at every turn: our ancient
relatives
walking towards us.

water sunk below porous rock
lime and chalk-filtered river
knows only the winter of the world
an inverse persephone
it rises from the dorset fields:
as harvest's daughter turns her back
the landscape cracks
and the running river ripples cold and clear
returning to its track
borne there by the winter.

yusuf dreams of drowning even when he wakes
was coming to this clouded chalkscape a

terrible mistake?
yusuf dreams of drowning now and not the
sound guns make
and the raindrops still don't silence the lives
distance takes
but at least now it's his lungs that cry and not
his heart that breaks.

everywhere, everywhere
there's not a drop to drink
everywhere. the bridge is gone.
the walls are falling down
the house is full of thick grey mud—
but the summer will bring drought, no doubt
while christmas spews this flood
through the vestigial remnants of a town:
we can't go on, can't go on
the house begins to stink
and not one southern accent cares.

silty thames once ran higher in the hills of
england's bones
thrust into the sweating south by the mega
glacier's freezing hand
and now norfolk's shores recede like hair to
bring the coast's kiss wetly home
and the river valley is on fire.

how long ago did the fens rise; how long ago

did the Wash cycle end
how many millennia since the broads were cut
how many shivering sodden ancestors huddled
in one soggy hut?
(did it always rain like this?)
forty days and forty nights drowned the
wretched earth
and god stretched out his hand and
nothing but Foulness, rising from the sand
and two of every last remaining survivor
denied passage on the boat
as the whole of sinking england fails to float.

slapton sands sank a thousand americans but
first
it claimed homes, throwing the ocean on the
land
slapton village: slipping by degrees
into the hungry maw of the southern sea
made ravenous by dredging sand.

everywhere, everywhere
we are going down
the deflated rubber lifeboat
washes up upon the shingle shore
twenty-five sodden unknown sailors
sail and breathe no more—
the lands that spat them out stripped
by death from their tired faces

robbed all traces of identity
brothers of a hundred thousand drownéd
english seamen
who hail from different places.

once the waters demanded blood.
heads. shields. now, instead
we give them flowers.
flowers to apologise. flowers
to cover for the guilt.
flowers to hide the froth, the stench
the isotypes unstable decaying in
the placid upland streams.
the dead sheep, like a remnant of that former
pious slaughter,
resting half in, half out of cold leat water.
golf balls, like roc's eggs.
the butchered bodies of trafficked girls,
young men who begged—pleaded—sank—
then floated, to the consternation of an unlucky
angler,
and stank.
magnets for fishing with. magnet fishers. dead
fish. swans, leaded and unleaded.
and shit. so much shit.
until the fleet is thick with it
until the humber is sunk under
until the fog on the tyne is solid
until the holy waters of the wells of glastonbury

Derek Des Anges

grow squalid
we shit
where we drink
and still we sink.

umar left his land—birmingham—
to lie for several years under a wet towel.
his lungs are filling now
they're always filling now
there are so many things no one has said
while he's gasping for air
so many questions
but not one *sorry*.

the national water board.
the nation's watery body.
the water on the table
under the table
is rising still;
it's plain where the floods will come
and they will.

through the deep steep valley carved by
cracking ice
more moons ago than minds can count
runs the dark brown lock of hair of tamar
goddess of the bronze moors
bronze lover of the atlantic
near-connector of the irish waters

to the french;
in bridged bondage still churning,
fat as a bear with leaping salmon,
carrying the storms' blessing down from the
hills
yearning
for the times when she was fed with reverence
instead of undiluted untreated human piss.

holy, holy are the waters of the chalice
of the white lady
of the baths
holy are the waters that spring up from the
rocks;
we have forgotten this
and we are lost.

water, water, everywhere
cascading through the roof.
cleaning out the gutters;
pouring through the sea wall
the barriers and the drains:
england's rivers will rise again.

yusuf dreamt, again, that he would drown:
he woke to grey foreign england and grey
foreign faces

and the rain came down.

runnymede

my how the rotten hours lie;
they promise they'll go meekly by
instead they lurk and crowd the light
and the days go sluggish to the end.

a great charter laid down on an eyot
observed by a yew tree in 1215, standing
in uninterested deep forest green;
the tree stands still, observing
a very different world.

the yew grew before such strife
continued to live a yewish life
and will remain until it does not
there upon the river's eyot.

the signatories of that charter sought
only to win. it is the fate of men;
they love to win. only to win. winning
battles, winning money, winning women,
winning friends; there is nothing but the
contest: and then for them all, winning ends.

no one escapes death. the men who signed
the men who fought, the ones who won
the ones who lost: all laid down and fed the

earth;
the yew is standing still.

my how the rotten liars lie; they twist the truth
and reckon the cost. it's all a game,
they play to win. let them.
the yew is standing still, and it will
until it does not, there upon the eyot.

my how the wretched die:
as inevitably as the victors,
and no more.

Derek Des Anges

the art

to live in a city is to live in-between
to love that city is—
the slur "liminal" is wrong
it is the *taint*
the perineum; the shore.

to love that city is to slide on the knife-edge
between the grief of continual loss
(as your favourite dance hall becomes
another victim of another wrecking ball)
and the delight of the new lover
(in scrubland opens a new museum
whose remits screams*: people like you*
yeah people like you
we love you too; we love you too)

to live in a city is an art:
you must learn new semiotics
the auguries of graffiti
the maps of ever-shifting blocked roads
the language of dodging.

to love in that city is also an art:
you are no longer two people on the desert
island
of the world's shittiest village—

no longer prisoners in the same cell.
anyone you love in a city, you have chosen to
love
so choose well.

to live in a city is the art of surrender
to the tides of humanity and the savage
dereliction
of what once constituted personal space:
it is the art of finding solitude
with your nose rammed into a stranger's neck;
it is the act of creating silence
in a crowd at 120 decibels;
it is the power that flows through you
when you discover that you are now
incapable of getting lost.

to love that city is to always be found:
it is the choice to be known, or to be invisible.
to bring meaning, whole and entire
to each microscopic interaction—
—and to create in each the curtailed ecosystem
of a stifled love affair.
to love that city is to know what it feels like
to note the fall of each sparrow
and to let them hit the ground
because the song demands it.

to live in a city, to love that city

is eight million epithets for every warm body
that passes regularly through your periphery;
it is i-spy with the language flags
on the baristas who could outfox you in sacred
tongues:
it is the potted life history of men
you will never see again at three or four A.M.
who just need to know someone is listening.
(he was a translator for the british army
in afghanistan; now he sells jewellery in
camden market:
it is hard. he wants you to write a book about
it).

to tend to that city is to redistribute the coins
you found in hampstead
into the pockets of the rough sleepers you meet
in hounslow;
it is to feed the pigeons of charing cross the
crumbs of the croissant you craved in camden
passage:
to tend to that city is to tape
on every high place
hand-penned signs
begging strangers to keep their hearts beating.

to love a city is to take the heart that feeds a
village
and clone it a hundred thousand times

until it refracts off the river's oily surface
until it shines; until the art that knits together
some single household
grows into something
divine.

www.ingramcontent.com/pod-product-compliance
Lightning Source LLC
Chambersburg PA
CBHW072004060426
42446CB00042B/1817